HOSIERS. HATTERS.

E. & E. MATTHEWS

273, HIGH STREET (near Hoe Street),

WALTHAMSTOW.

UP-TO-DATE · GENT.'S · OUTFITTERS.

WE · CARRY · A · COMPLETE MODERN · STOCK · OF HIGH-CLASS · GOODS · WHICH WILL · APPEAL · PARTICULARLY · TO · THE WELL-DRESSED · MAN.

SHIRTS · MADE · TO · MEASURE · A · SPECIALITY.

Advertisement published in the Walthamstow Urban District Council "Borough" Guide 1911-1912.

"Shoppers Paradise"

A History of High Street Walthamstow

by

J W Howes, F.L.A.

and

A D Law, A.M.A.

c/o Vestry House Museum, Vestry Road,
Walthamstow, London E17 9NH

Monograph (New Series) No. 28
1991
Reprinted 1996
ISBN 085480 047 6
Printed by Intercity Print Financial PLC
Reprinted by Walthamstow Historical Society 2002

Cover illustration:
High Street, from corner of Blackhorse Road, c.1900

Introduction

The booklet entitled 'Memories of High Street', which was originally published in 1977 and reprinted in 1988, has evoked sufficient interest to motivate the authors to research and publish this introductory history relating to the High Street.

The High Street has changed considerably throughout the course of this century and is ever changing. The important archive deposited at Vestry House Museum and the recent photographic survey undertaken by the Waltham Forest In Focus group are crucial in both preserving material and recording the development of High Street respectively.

A debt of gratitude for the production of this booklet is owed to the staff of Vestry House Museum and particularly to Mrs Maureen Newton for efficiently presenting the text in a form suitable for publication. Appreciation is also accorded to Mr Walter H Bowyer, Mr Roger J Colori and Mrs Winifred I Ellingham for their wise and valued counsel.

H Martin Stuchfield
Hon Secretary
Walthamstow Historical Society

Marsh Street, Walthamstow (top end), 1860.
The Houses left to right are: Longdale House (No. 221 behind trees - later the gas showrooms; Clevelands (No. 223 - later education offices); Elm House (No. 225 - later the Conservative Club); Mansfield House (No. 227 - became shops); Eastfield Lodge (No. 229 - became a bank and a drapers).

High Street opposite Westbury Road, 1913.

CHAPTER ONE

Marsh Street is renamed

On the 22nd December 1882 the Walthamstow Board of Health[1] decided to change the name of a once rural road leading from Hoe Street down to the Lea marshes, from Marsh Street to High Street. This seemingly unimportant administrative action certainly indicates that by the late 19th century the town already had a generally accepted main shopping street. The story of High Street must therefore paradoxically begin by outlining the history of a road of an entirely different name!

Marsh Street ran from the higher ground around the older Walthamstow village area down to the damp and fairly remote marsh along the banks of the river Lea. It was never an important road, the main routes to and from London being Lea Bridge Road or Mill (later Ferry) Lane. During the 17th century land at the eastern end of the road (well away from the marshes), was purchased by various fairly wealthy city merchants seeking sites to build 'country retreats' in the then rural quietude of Walthamstow; an area within daily reach of the City by horse coach or in their own carriages. Residents included two Admirals, Sir William Batten and Sir William Penn whose more famous son founded Pennsylvania. Another was Doctor Daniel Whistler, the first person to identify ricketts as a disease (ironically a disease from which many poor children in Walthamstow would suffer in the 19th and early 20th centuries).

At the lower end of the street, both geographically and socially, there were at that time groups of small cheaply constructed cottages some occupied by workers employed at the watermill which was then sited at the end of the present Coppermill Lane. It is also probable that others living in these more humble buildings worked as domestic servants in the aforementioned larger houses but there are no records to substantiate this.

At the end of the 17th century and throughout the 18th, most of the large houses were for various reasons demolished and smaller ones built, albeit (by modern standards) still quite large establishments staffed by several servants and having extensive well cared for gardens.

To one such house came Fanny Keats, aged 12, sister of John Keats, to live with her guardian Richard Abbey, she and her brother having been orphaned at an early age. Fanny attended two schools in Marsh Street (Miss Caley's and Miss Tuckey's) from 1814 until the end of 1818. Fanny was certainly not very happy living in Marsh Street and in later years wrote that:

The Chequers public house, c.1968.

"My guardian was not too careful of me, always kept me a prisoner, having no other acquaintances than my books, birds and flowers".

Visits from her brother do not seem to have been encouraged but he did write to her and occasionally *walked* over from Hampstead to see her. The Abbeys gave Fanny no money of her own but John did what he could to brighten her lonely life by bringing her roots and seeds for her small personal garden, until his untimely death in 1821 aged only 25. When she became of age (21) Fanny left Marsh Street, Walthamstow, and the Abbey family, no doubt with some relief, and never returned!

Sad though the life of young Fanny Keats was in Marsh Street, other young children suffered far more in the elegant houses similar to the one in which she lived, these were the 'Climbing Boys'. The large chimneys of such houses were often cleaned by sending small boys up or down them to sweep away the soot. In 1824 in the 'Chimney-Sweepers Friend and Climbing Boys Album' it was recorded that:

"In the beginning of the year 1808, a chimney-sweeper's boy being employed to sweep a chimney in Marsh Street, Walthamstow, in the house of Mr. Jeffery, carpenter, unfortunately in his attempt to get down, stuck in the flue, and was unable to extricate himself. Mrs. Jeffery, being within hearing of the boy, immediately procured assistance. As the chimney was low, and the top of it easily accessible from without, the boy was taken out in about ten minutes, the chimney-pot and several rows of bricks having been previously removed. If he had remained in that dreadful situation many minutes longer, he must have died. His master was sent for, and he arrived soon after the boy had been released. He abused him for the accident, and after striking him, sent him with a bag of soot to sweep another chimney. The child appeared so very weak when taken out that he could scarcely stand, and yet this wretched being, who had been up ever since three o'clock, had before been sent by his master to Wanstead, which, with his walk to Marsh Street, made about 5 miles. This, incidentally, is one of the mildest cases recorded."

It is pleasing to note in a Walthamstow Historical Society publication that because of this and other similar incidents throughout the country, groups were formed to stop this practice and the first practical folding flexible chimney brush was invented by a Walthamstow resident.[2]

The social distinctions between the higher and lower ends of the streets were also reflected in two public houses, the 'Chequers' and the 'Cock'. The 'Chequers' was patronised by the more affluent and the 'Cock' (replaced by the present Victorian pub designed by T. W. Fletcher), by the then termed 'lower orders'.

It is recorded that the 'Chequers' was often used in the 18th century by the local Vestry when money matters were being dealt with. This was common practice during the period and is one of several reasons given for naming public houses 'The Chequers'. The landlords provided simple primitive calculators using a chequer board (hence 'exchequer') and members of the Vestry availed themselves of the food and drink readily provided.

Religious life in the Street was confined to the activities of various dissenting congregations, and the growth of local protestant nonconformity, so excellently reviewed by M.E. Batsford in 'Non-Conformity in Walthamstow',[3] could be said to have originated in Marsh Street in 1672. In that year Revd Samuel Slater, who had been ejected from his living in Bury St Edmunds for refusing to comply with the 1662 Act of Uniformity, came to live in Marsh Street and was given a licence to use his house for 'Presbyterian Meetings'. Records indicate that his own congregation did not thrive but nevertheless by 1690 the number of dissenters in Walthamstow had greatly increased. To meet their need for a proper meeting place William Coward, a wealthy dissenting merchant living in 'Cleveland' (a house once sited almost opposite the present Central Library), built in 1695 a place of worship virtually in his garden. This building became known as the 'Old Meeting"and soon attracted such large congregations that in 1793 a larger building had to be erected on the same site. To this came Dr Isaac Watts and Dr Philip Doddridge both well known hymn writers who were friends of Coward and stayed at his house.

Marsh Street Congregational Church prior to demolition in 1965.

However, towards the end of the 18th century there had been a split in the congregation of the 'Old Meeting' because some members objected to the 'Unitarian' views of the then minister. Those who so objected moved out of the 'Old Meeting' to a building erected in 1787 lower down Marsh Street near to the present Willow Walk. To the confusion of future historians this became known as the 'New Meeting'. It prospered under its ministers as did the 'Old Meeting' under the highly esteemed Dr Eliezer Cogan from 1801-1816 when he also managed a school at Essex Hall in Higham Hill. When Dr Cogan left, the congregation for various reasons declined and the 'Old Meeting' building was finally demolished in 1861.

Ironically (and confusingly) the 'New Meeting' at the same time had increased its congregation to about 500 and seeking a site for a new church was able to purchase the site vacated by the 'Old Meeting', where in 1871 it erected a gothic style church designed by John Tarring & Son. The steeple of this building dominated the skyline of High Street until it was damaged by a flying bomb in 1944. By 1965 the congregation had declined so much that the church was demolished and shops built on the site. Members of the church joined the Trinity Congregational Church in Orford Road, which then became Marsh Street Trinity Church, The 'Marsh Street' part of the title was retained when in 1972 the church became part of the United Reformed Church, thus keeping alive the original name of High Street.

The building near Willow Walk which the 'New Meeting' vacated was eventually sold to the Primitive Methodists in 1875 and survived until 1977. This church had its own burial ground at the rear, which, until it was built over, contained the grave of a refugee from religious persecution in Madagascar in the 1840's, brought to England by a local Missionary. The interior of the building had been altered over the years but photographs show that before demolition it was still attractive with fine cast iron decoration on the front of the balcony which itself was supported by delicate cast iron columns. It was a good example of the simple 'preaching boxes' the early non-conformists built; buildings which are only now being appreciated for their definite architectural merit.

Whilst nothing remains of the Primitive Methodist Church a school founded by the Marsh Street Congregations in 1838 when they used the building still exists at Sevenoaks, Kent. This is the 'Walthamstow Hall School' which moved there in 1882. The original school was established for the daughters of missionaries in a house that stood near Mission Grove. This provision was obviously needed as in 1841 another school was opened to provide a 'Home and School for the sons of Missionaries', which eventually became Eltham College at Mottingham, Kent.

The old burial ground at the rear of the High Street Methodist Church which was built over following demolition of the church in 1977.

High Street, 1907. Looking westwards with the entrance to Northcott House on the right.

The religious High Street building with the most colourful past must be the Salvation Army Citadel, the name of which can still be seen above No. 99A. It was built between 1891 and 1892, ironically on the site of Ball's boxing booths. Designed by W. Gilbee Scott, the few remaining photographs indicate that the interior must have been almost a 'theatre in the round' with balconies decorated with charming fretted wooden valances. According to a contemporary report the building's opening was 'celebrated by having a number of girls dressed in art muslin of various colours riding about the streets in hansom cabs'. By 1903 the congregation had grown to 932 making it the second largest non-conformist group in the town, rivalled only by the 'Lighthouse' in Markhouse Road. The 'Army' bands were a regular feature of High Street and it is certain that Salvationists visited the 'Cock' and 'Chequers' to sell 'War Cry' and talk about the evils of drink to customers. It was not until as late as 1958 that the 'Army' left High Street to take over the former Lloyd Park Methodist church and the 'Citadel' was converted into a shop and storage area.

Thus High Street could certainly be called the birthplace of non-conformity in Walthamstow, but apart from the Salvation Army Citadel facade, little remains to record this fact. The street is now completely 'secular' apart from the occasional religious haranguing of evangelical groups trying to be heard above the cries of the stall holders and the sounds of the shopping crowds.

CHAPTER TWO

19th and early 20th Centuries 'The Longest Street Market'

The railway came to St. James Street and Hoe Street (now Walthamstow Central)[4] station in 1870 but several years before this speculative builders had begun to transform the area on either side of Marsh Street by building rows of smaller houses for rent or sale. Many of these roads exist to this day although some were demolished when the new shopping precinct was built. The coming of the railway nevertheless encouraged even greater building activity so that by 1882 when 'Marsh Street' became 'High Street' the larger houses were already being demolished or adapted to form shops in the new shopping street. Only one of these large houses remains and this can be seen above the facade of the former gas showrooms at the corner of Cleveland Park Avenue.[5]

Bricks for building houses were usually made on the site using the easily available local clay. Kilns were built prior to building and once sufficient bricks had been produced the kilns would be destroyed and new ones built wherever the next row of houses was to be erected. Bankruptcy was common amongst builders but in spite of allegations of 'Jerry' building[6] the majority of the houses were well built and survive to this day.

High Street, as we can now call it, still remained however almost a village shopping centre and a contemporary writer lauded the fact that "a shop keeper still has time to water his forecourt on a hot summer's day". The watering being needed to 'lay the dust' rising from a then still untarmacadamed surface of the street.

It was not until 1885 that there is a record of stalls being set up in High Street, but five years later in 1890 regulations had to be drawn up to prevent fights between potential stall holders trying to obtain the best sites. Stalls were not allowed to be erected before 8 a.m. but intending stall holders still waited in side streets and at the stipulated hour rushed out to stake their claim.

At this time the stalls would have been simple easily transportable tables, or 'coster' barrows, carried or pushed to the market. Later stalls were built up on flat topped hand carts evolving eventually into the traditional market stall often with twisted brass rods supporting a framework onto which a canvas cover could be fitted. The wheels would be carved and decorated and the name of the trader displayed on a finely signed board hanging above the goods on display. Unfortunately few of these have survived.

Some means of illuminating stalls was required once the market began to stay open later and at first this was supplied by crude naphtha flares and then well designed pressure 'Tilley' type lamps were introduced which gave a far better light, although this must have been none too flattering to food on display!

The growing number of shops and stalls did not however serve only the comparatively well paid clerks, compositors and similar workers who purchased or more likely, rented, the new houses being built, they also served a growing number of poor in the town. One type of shop in particular met their needs, the Pawn Shop. On Monday mornings queues, mainly of women, would form outside the door of the Pledge Office; a door often discreetly hidden at the side of the main shop to keep those buying jewellery and watches well away from those about to pawn or redeem goods.

All kinds of goods would be pawned even sheets and blankets to raise money to pay rent, buy food, light and heating. If all went well the items would be redeemed on the Friday night when the husbands had been paid. To record the items pawned 'pawn tickets' were issued and Vestry House Museum was presented by one local pawnbroker with a wonderful 'Heath Robinson' contraption designed in the late 19th century, to write out several identical tickets at once before carbon paper became widely available.

The atmosphere of High Street in the 1920's and 30's, its characters and sights are well recorded in the companion volume 'Memories of High Street', but between 1900 and 1914 it already had much to interest the shopper apart from the stalls. One local resident wrote:

'Naphtha lighting shed a fitful, stinking, spluttering glow until at least midnight on Saturdays. You could, within a few yards, buy a pet, have a tooth pulled, fill your market bag with shopping for sixpence, adorn yourself with a "genuine" Indian scent, safeguard yourself with a bottle of a "wonder cure-all", have a bunion removed, be weighed, be measured and be robbed. Over all was the ever present smell and noise. The smell came from the rubbish piled ankle-deep in the gutters, spoiled eggs, discarded fish, smelling salts, cheese, second-hand clothing, third-hand shoes, saveloys, faggots, hot potatoes, hokey pokey ice cream, cough candies, hot fritters and jars of pickled fish. The noise came from the stall holders and the crowd. The yells of the competing traders, the answers of the bargain hunters, the hoarse patter of the 'quacks', the delight of the 'cured', the flash talk of the swindlers and the angry complaints of the swindled! It was an angry, tumultuous scene of supply and demand!'

They had their characters before the First World War as well as in the 20's and 30's, possibly even more outlandish ones! 'Old Bogey' for example, was a colourful drunkard who spent his time avoiding two groups of people; the police who often led him drunk into a Police Station cell and the Salvation Army who saw in him a very real challenge! The latter, it is recorded, won and he ended his years carrying the Army banner on parades down High Street.

An Italian photographer named Matioli attracted custom by dressing his sons in weird military uniforms of obscure states and a George Borwick, of 'Borwick's baking powder' fame, first sold his product on a stall at this time. Even a 'medicine man' dressed as a Wild West marshal, kept a stall for some years, selling cures based on rhubarb plants.

76 High Street, 1989. L.Manze's Pie and Mash Shop with Mrs K Nicholls, Miss T Nicholls and Mr F Nicholls (Manager).

(Waltham Forest In Focus)

The Clare family say goodbye to their fish stall in the High Street after 67 years, April 1974. The business was started by Wally Clare and carried on by his son Alfred.
(Waltham Forest Guardian)

114 High Street, 1960. Fish Bros. Limited, Jewellers and Pawnbrokers.
(Walthamstow Guardian)

On the site, where the Salvation Army Citadel was later to be erected, one Alf Ball managed a small show ground with boxing booths that were famous throughout the 'East End'. Bouts were held between professional fighters and volunteers hoping to win a useful 'purse', which they seldom did.

By 1890 the booths appear to have been in decline and a pathetic attempt was made to revive support by showing a boxing lion. An aged lion from a circus had gloves fitted to its front paws and a boxer would enter its cage and punch the poor beast to make it at least snarl. Thankfully this sad 'entertainment' failed to draw audiences and the booths closed. The site was sold to the Salvation Army who in 1891 started to erect a 'Citadel' on it.

When war broke out in 1914 some of the stallholders and shopkeepers with even the slightest of German sounding names were attacked by rioters and their goods stolen or destroyed. Similar actions took place throughout the country, but this does not excuse what took place in Walthamstow High Street and elsewhere in the town. Eventually such anti-social activity ceased and the market continued to grow peacefully, apart from a rash of anti-semitic demonstrations in the 1930's. A yearly increasing demand for stall sites, which were still on the 'first come' basis often resulted in quite serious fighting between rivals for the best sites. In 1932 the Borough Council took action and introduced a system which licensed stall holders and leased to them definite numbered sites indicated by metal plates set into the surface of the road. The income from the license fees was, and still is, used to clear up the street after the market closes. By these actions the disputes over sites was ended and most of the smells and rubbish often mentioned in early writings were removed soon after the market closed.

The majority of the early shops in the street were owned by local people, the largest being Lidstone's opened at the junction with Pretoria Avenue. This was for some years the grandest shop in the area and was festooned with a complex miniature aerial ropeway to take cash to, and change from, a cashier sited in a control box in the centre of the store. A system remembered with delight by those who knew the shop when they were children.

Few such 'family' shops continue to trade today. Howard's 'Dolls Hospital' which traded near the Palmerston Road junction has long closed; modern dolls seeming no longer to need eyes, legs, arms, or even heads replaced! Fish Bros. (No. 114) one of the early shops however is still in existence at the time of publication.

18 High Street, c.1910. J Sainsbury.

19 High Street, c.1905. After being bought in 1914 from the London Penny Bazaar, it was opened as a Marks & Spencer store. Closed in 1931 when a branch was opened at 43-47 High Street. (Marks & Spencer)

High Street at the junction with Blackhorse Road, 1964.
The store of F W Woolworth & Co. Ltd. was demolished in 1974.

7-9 High Street, 1963. The new Co-op supermarket on the corner of Pretoria Avenue preparing for opening. *(Walthamstow Guardian)*

High Street, once it was established as a market, soon attracted what in the early part of the century were called 'chain' stores, such as Woolworths and Marks & Spencer together with 'chain' grocers trading as Home & Colonial, Liptons, Maypole and Williams stores, together with Sainsbury's, which still has a High Street branch.

A Woolworth's was built in 1916 at the corner of Blackhorse Road, and twice enlarged in the 1930's, originally trading as the '3d and 6d' store (i.e. three and six old pennies). Close by at the corner of Pretoria Avenue, opposite Lidstone's, at No. 19 was a 'London Penny Bazaar', then a cheaper version of Woolworths. In 1914 Marks & Spencer took over the shop and traded there until 1931.

Surprisingly, High Street has never boasted even one really large department store. Until the construction of the Selborne Shopping Precinct, it remained, as it began, a street of individual shops possibly adding to its atmosphere and attracting mainly local shoppers, even when boosted by the London Tourist Board as 'England's Longest Street Market'.

The Second World War naturally led to restrictions of the opening hours of both shops and stalls, especially the latter which could not display any form of lighting during black-out hours. As a result the public became used to the shorter hours and it is only recently that the trend to late-night shopping has been re-established. High Street suffered from bombings as did the rest of the Borough although from details published in 'The War Over Walthamstow'[7] only a few high explosive bombs fell in the actual street; a pair falling on Friday, 27 December, 1940, demolishing numbers 130-4 and causing casualties and one death. The worst incident took place on the 16 August, 1944, just north of High Street where it joins Hoe Street. It was at 10 a.m. that a flying bomb fell close to Stoffer's fish shop which, as fish was in short supply, was crowded. There were over 144 casualties including 22 deaths, one of the worst incidents in the locality. However, even whilst bombs, Vl's and V2's were falling, plans were being drawn up for an improved High Street, not eventually realised until over 40 years later.

CHAPTER THREE

Civic Pride

With the rapid population growth of Walthamstow, there came increased demands from residents for the provision of local amenities such as libraries, public baths and schools. Wisely the Urban District Council, established in 1895, decided to site such facilities in the busiest part of the town, namely High Street.

However, the Local Board had not been totally inactive in the previous years, providing two most important amenities for a busy shopping area, a public 'automatic flushing urinal' in 1891, and in 1892 the town's first public library.

The location of the public urinal has been difficult to trace, but there can be no doubt about the site of the original library! This was a large house called 'Rosebank' which stood almost exactly where the present Central Library stands. Public Libraries could then only be established if the majority of local residents voted to adopt the relevant Act and this Walthamstow residents overwhelmingly did. 'Rosebank' soon became inadequate for the heavy demands made upon it and a large reading room was built behind the house and opened on the 29 September 1894. This fine example of Victorian architecture is now the main lending library for the Borough, its excellent plasterwork having been completely replaced after the disastrous fire of 1982. Soon even these facilities were too small for the town and approaches were made to the American philanthropist Andrew Carnegie to finance the building of a new library. Carnegie had educated himself using public libraries and museums and because of this established a trust to help such institutions. The trust would pay for the building, but the local residents had to pay for staff and books.

In 1907 a grant of £10,000 was made to the Urban District Council and soon plans for a new library were being drawn up. The architect was J.Williams Dunsford, a fairly prolific, if minor architect, who designed a series of local authority buildings, usually in the 'Queen Anne' style. He excelled himself in Walthamstow, producing a building which Sir Nikolaus Pevsner in the Essex volume of the 'Buildings of England' called "A building in the pretty, somewhat mixed style of the day which was so often and successfully used for small municipal buildings". Fortunately, this delightful building escaped damage from the fire of 1982 and is now 'Listed' as being of 'outstanding architectural and historical interest'.

The opening of the High Street public library on 10th July 1909.

The new building contained a lecture hall which was immensely popular for many years after it was opened. In 1908 for example, thirty-one lectures, a concert and three exhibitions were held there, attracting over 45,000 people. During the First World War the hall served as an emergency hospital ward for the expected influx of casualties. After the war interest in public lectures declined, whilst the need for a large reference library for the town increased. The lecture hall was ideal for this purpose and many who used it from the 1920's onwards possibly thought this was the purpose for which it was designed.

In the 1920's the 'reading room' was converted into a lending library and in the 1930's a mezzanine floor was built inside this almost doubling the amount of shelving and as a result the number of books available. This remains the main lending library for the Borough, although it has been modernised after fire almost destroyed both the building and books.

The fire was deliberately started late on the evening of Saturday, 27 February 1982, by arsonists who broke into the building and planted crude (but effective) incendiary devices at strategic places. Had the fire not been spotted by a local resident at about 10.45 p.m. the Central Library would

The Public Baths in the High Street, c.1900-1909. Opened on 28th July 1900 the building was used as a Public Hall during the winter months with dances, lectures, concerts, dinners, film shows and meetings of all kinds held.

have been completely destroyed. In the event the fine Victorian hall containing the lending library suffered most, especially the Music and Record Library where one of the best lending libraries of musical scores in outer London was destroyed together with several thousand L.P. recordings. The rest of the lending section was blackened with soot and the fine decorative plaster details on the roof made so dangerous that they had to be completely removed and replaced with copies when the restoration of the hall was undertaken. The outstanding main staircase of the building was also damaged beyond repair and this too had to be rebuilt. Fortunately the reference library/lecture hall and offices in the front part of the building were untouched by fire. The restoration work took nearly two years to complete and involved many fine craftsmen to copy the original Victorian details which were such an attractive feature of the library.

A tribute should here be recorded to the library staff who worked for weeks in filthy conditions to rescue and clean the more valuable books that could be saved for further use and established an emergency service to the public which opened soon after the fire. From the public outcry following the fire it was obvious that the Central Library was highly regarded by local residents, a fact that must have helped towards the decision to build a further extension.

Attractive as it was, a Reference Library sited on the first floor was inconvenient for many and hindered the development of a much needed public information service. A bid was therefore made for funds to be made available by the developers of the Selborne Shopping Precinct to compensate for the loss of some public facilities in the area. The Council supported the proposals to build an extension to the Central Library from this money thus providing easier access to the Lending and Reference Libraries whilst preserving the attractive exterior of the main building. Unfortunately following the fire the vacated first floor Reference Library had to be used as offices and storage, but it is hoped that eventually this fine auditorium will be made available as a much needed venue for talks, concerts and similar public meetings, the purpose for which it was designed.

Whilst reading was considered important by the early Town Council, they did not forget more mundane matters. Swimming was popular and as few houses had bathrooms 'slipper' baths were needed too. To meet these two needs public baths were built next to the library. The swimming bath was formally opened on the 21st December 1903 by a hardy gentleman who dived through a paper hoop into the slightly heated water a performance perhaps more suited to the circus and one rather lacking in civic dignity. The swimming pool provided recreation and the 'slipper' baths - (1st and 2nd class) cleanliness. You could not turn on either the hot or cold bath water yourself, an attendant did this by remote control presumably guided by the screams of the alternatively scalded or frozen bathers!

The swimming bath was entered by an immaculate white painted ticket hall with shining brass fittings reminiscent of an early steam ship. The air, full of the smell of coarse freshly laundered white towels, soap and chlorine.

On either side of the pool miniature 'horse-boxes' served as changing rooms - ladies one side, gents the other. Sometimes waves made by about 100 school children splashing around caused the water to overflow under the main doors and down High Street. You had, however, to behave in the baths as amongst the rules it was clearly stated:

1. A person resorting to the baths shall not knowingly intrude upon or interfere with the privacy of any other person using any bath-room or any dressing-room.

2. A person resorting to the baths shall not cause any dog belonging to him, or under his control to enter or remain in any bath.

3. Any person resorting to the baths shall not while being in any swimming bath use any soap or other substance or preparation whereby the water may be rendered turbid or unfit for the use of bathers.

In the winter the pool was covered and dances, concerts and political meetings were held, a regular event being the annual Police concert, later facilities for indoor bowls were provided. Here some of the first crude film shows were given in the town, some of them photographed at Higham Hill. The Baths continued to serve the Borough until the new baths were opened in Chingford Road.

A growing population also needed schools other than those provided by various religious denominations. The passing of the 'Mundella Act' in 1880 was the culmination of the pioneer Forster Education Act of 1870. For the first time education was compulsory for children albeit only from the age of 5 to 10, after which it was possible to obtain exemption providing certain standards had been reached, and full time education ended for all at 14. To meet the requirements of this Act, local School Boards were set up in all major towns and eventually the Walthamstow Education Offices took over one of the remaining Georgian houses at the eastern (Hoe Street) end of High Street, called 'Clevelands' and remained there until the new Town Hall in Forest Road opened in 1941.

Several schools had existed in High Street as mentioned in Chapter 1, but only one was still functioning when the 1880 Act came into force.This was the Marsh Street (later British) school founded in 1789 by a group of dissenters, a school which occupied various small buildings close to the junction of High Street and Buxton Road, before it occupied a purpose built school in the same location in 1872. In 1881 the school was transferred to the School Board and eventually another larger school was built 'Marsh Street School' which remained standing until the building of the present Sainsbury's. It closed as a school in 1932 but remained in use as a Youth Club and Library until demolished in 1979.

Another purpose built school is still standing - Mission Grove. Erected in 1906, this, like the Central Library, was built in the 'Queen Anne' style but on a more modest scale. However, it is an interesting building as it reflects the 'secular' nature of Board School education which led the leading architects of Board Schools to eschew any features that could be seen as 'ecclesiastical', e.g. Gothic windows.

In 1889 the long established Sir George Monoux Grammar School moved into a newly built school in High Street, but until 1916 it remained independent of the local School Board. Whatever its previous scholastic standards, an inquiry in 1906 found 'the teaching ineffective, the curriculum wrong and the supply of books and equipment poor'. However it was not until 1916 that the school was taken over by Essex County Council which was then the relevant body for secondary education. In 1932 the school transferred to its present buildings in Chingford Road and the Old Monoux School served as various municipal offices until it was demolished in November 1984.

The school must have been a very noisy place for the pupils and one, James Hilton, the novelist and playwright, remembered the smells of Gillard's pickle factory (opposite the school) permeating the rooms and adding to the distractions of the cries of the stall holders.

One other school should be mentioned, known locally as the 'Truant School' housed in a rather good Georgian house, No. 115 on the west side of the junction with Palmerston Road. Built in the 1750's the house had a very fine doorway, a feature not likely to be appreciated by the boys sent there!

In 1908 another important service was provided by the Urban District Council, namely a new public convenience. This was buried below ground level, presumably to hide it away from prudish passers by. Nevertheless unlike the first such provision both sexes were catered for and the convenience remained in use until 1956 when new facilities at ground level were erected in Selborne Park. The old convenience was then filled with rubble and cemented over, possibly providing future archaeologists with interesting details of life in the early 20th century!

There was limited public transport along High street over the years although horse and later motor buses did use the street until 1906 when a serious accident involving a motor bus the previous year, caused a total ban on such services. Trams were never officially used in the street but at the notorious 'S' bend at the junction with Blackhorse Road, they would frequently jump the track and become well and truly stuck in the surface of High Street causing long hold ups for the even limited traffic of the time.

Finally, mention must be made of another service provided in the street, first by volunteers, and then by the Urban District Council; a fire service.

In 1894 a fire station was built at No. 116 manned by volunteers until 1897 when a full time service was financed by the Council. In retrospect the siting of the baths, library and schools seems to have been wise, but placing a fire station in the centre of an ever busier shopping street lined with market stalls was certainly unwise, if not sheer folly! Stalls were often overturned when the engine raced out from the station scattering people and goods in its wake. Common sense prevailed in 1924 when a new fire station was built in Forest Road and relative peace returned to High Street.

Today only the Central Library remains as a visible reminder of the varied examples of 'Civic Pride' that once added to the attractions of High Street. Fortunately it is a fine building in an ideal site for a busy library and when, eventually, the lecture room is again available for public use, the town should regain the use of an excellent auditorium.

High Street (Central) public library, c.1913.

The Carlton Cinema, c.1962. The cinema closed on 28th March 1964 and was incorporated into a Tesco supermarket prior to demolition.

CHAPTER FOUR

Walthamstow's first Leisure Centre

The early years of this century witnessed the establishing of the main centre of entertainment for the town in High Street. The street becoming the obvious venue for a 'night out' coupled with a good 'blow out', of jellied eels and mash from Manzes, hot saveloys and pease pudding from the butchers, or roasted potatoes from one of the small coke ovens on wheels serving these precursors of modern 'fast food'.

If for example you wanted to 'go to the pictures' you had the choice of two large cinemas the 'Prince's Pavilion' or the 'Carlton'. For a short time there was one other, the 'Royal', but as this only survived less than a year, opening at 203 High Street on Boxing Day 1911 and closing in April 1912, it need not be considered in detail. It is likely that it was just a rather grand 'side-show' in a shop, a left-over from the days of the early bioscope shows seen at fair grounds.

'The Prince's Pavilion', on the site of the present 'Dominion Mecca Bingo Hall' started showing films in 1909 and obviously this was popular as in 1912 it was rebuilt providing Walthamstow with its first purpose-built cinema. It must have been quite spacious for the period, seating 1,000, and was 'large and roomy so that everyone can see the screen with a clear view'. From contemporary accounts the interior was rather spartan, with wooden benches in front and a little more comfortable tip-up seats at the rear. Decoration was almost non-existent, the roof girders being exposed and clusters of bare electric lamps providing illumination when required. The entrances and exits were also tucked away at one side, opening onto a passageway.

The other purpose-built cinema was the 'Carlton' which opened only two years later on 13 November 1913, and was far more luxurious. Designed by the same architect as the Central Library, J. Williams Dunsford, its entrance was 'richly carpeted having oak panelled walls and antique lanterns and illuminations'. The auditorium was also a great advance on the 'Prince's' and when in 1925 a large pipe organ was installed with ranks of pipes on either side of the screen it must have been quite impressive. The organ however, could never be used at full volume as this caused large pieces of plasterwork to drop on to the audiences! The purpose of the organ was to replace the small 'Carlton Orchestra' of six players that had provided a musical background to silent films. The cinema was never rebuilt although it was refurbished in 1959, finally closing in March 1964 to be converted into a supermarket, chemists and then a Tesco store, later demolished when the Selborne Walk Shopping Centre was built.

In May 1930 the 'Prince's' was demolished, the age of the 'super' cinema having arrived. It was replaced by the 'Dominion' cinema designed by Clifford Aish, seating 1,685 patrons, more than half the number that could be seated in its nearest rival, the 'Granada' in Hoe Street. The owners however, drew attention to the building's "restrained tasteful decor unlike many other large cinemas". The entrance hall nevertheless sported 'Venetian' lanterns and vaguely baroque plaster work, although the auditorium was 'Art Deco' and almost stark when compared with the exuberant Spanish interior of the 'Granada'. It was opened on 22 December 1930 in dense fog which prevented many of the invited guests reaching the cinema, and never established itself as a local 'institution' as did the 'Granada' in Hoe Street.

The 'Dominion' had however, one feature to rival the 'Granada', a genuine 'Wurlitzer' cinema organ built in the United States. Although the trade name 'Wurlitzer' is often applied to cinema organs in general, real 'Wurlitzers' were comparatively rare in England as there were several other makers supplying organs for cinemas. Such organs were already an anachronism in the 1930's, as sound films had taken over from silent films more quickly than was expected whilst new cinemas had been planned on the assumption that most films would still be silent. As a result to get at least some return for a very expensive item, a short organ recital was a regular feature of cinema programmes before the Second World War and shortly after. Some 78 r.p.m. recordings were made of the Dominion 'Wurlitzer' and there were recitals by visiting organists such as the then famous Sidney Torch. The organ was eventually sold to Alfred E. Davies & Son Ltd., of Northampton in 1958 who are likely to have broken it down to provide spare parts for other organs. Nothing remains of this form of entertainment in High Street, but at least the 'Christie' organ in the Granada has been lovingly restored by organ enthusiasts and can be heard from time to time.

Live entertainment could also be had at the 'Palace Theatre', built in 1903 to designs by Wylson & Long and opened on the 28 December 1903. The interior was typical of the Theatre Royal, Stratford or the Hackney Empire. In addition to the stalls and pit there was a balcony (or circle), above that a gallery and on either side of the proscenium arch two boxes. Those sitting on the hard benches in the gallery must have been frequently tempted to drop orange peel, apple cores and other missiles on the more affluent below as to prevent this a wire mesh was erected completely along the front of the 'Gods'.

The opening programme was given by Fred Karno's company, a troupe in which the then young Charles Chaplin performed. Most of the great stars of the music hall appeared at the 'Palace' making the rounds of the music halls of East London in their own carriages, sometimes appearing four or five times at different venues on one night. These were performers such as Harry Champion, Harry Lauder, Marie Lloyd, Gus Elen and Gertie Gitana, who were soon to become forgotten as the newer stars of the silent cinema attracted the audience that once queued to see and hear them.

The 'Palace' was able to compete with the cinema during the 20's and 30's, staging regular variety shows twice nightly and an annual circus and pantomime. After the Second World War it was reduced to including semi-nude shows to attract audiences, with little effect on their decline, either numerically or morally. In 1952 the Countess de la Marr took over the theatre with the aim of presenting plays instead of variety shows. This well intended revival failed to attract larger audiences and on the 20 February 1954 the last curtain fell in the 'Palace' at the end of a poorly attended performance of 'Desire under the Elms'. By 1960 the building had become derelict and was demolished in the same year. Now only the 'Palace Parade' of shops remains as a reminder of a once popular venue for a 'good night out'.

Two other venues for those seeking convivial company existed in High Street at the same time as the cinemas and theatre, the Workingmen's Club and the Conservative Club. The former was one of the first such clubs founded in London being formed in 1862. It occupied (and still occupies) a building down a small passage almost opposite Mission Grove, but its once delightfully decorated entrance has been destroyed. The Conservative Club occupied two Georgian houses at the higher end of High Street until 1960 when the houses were demolished and the club moved to Church Lane.

Nothing, apart from a cinema made into a bingo hall, now remains of the hey-day of entertainment in High Street, a time when it was truly the 'centre of town'. Fortunately old programmes, posters and photographs are preserved at Vestry House Museum and excellent accounts of the buildings mentioned are contained in Greg Tonkins booklet 'Showtime in Walthamstow'.[8] In addition the memories of those who attended the cinemas and theatre are recorded in the companion volume to this, 'Memories of High Street'. Live entertainment is still however provided by the traditionally loquacious stall holders selling their wares and indulging in lively Cockney repartee with customers and each other. The buildings may have gone but on a busy market day entertainment can still be found in High Street and a 'good blow out' enjoyed in the splendid untouched tiled interior of Manzes eel and pie shop.

Looking down High Street from the corner of Central Parade, 1963.
(Walthamstow Guardian)

Bonner's fruit stall near 228 High Street, 1989. A general shopping scene.
(Waltham Forest In Focus)

CHAPTER FIVE

Doing the 'Selborne Walk'

In spite of years of planning it was not until 1979 that developers were invited to submit plans and tenders for the improvement of the eastern (Hoe Street) end of High Street. In the event the delay may have been fortunate as for many years after the war car parking was seldom taken into account when planning a shopping area and the Victoria Line certainly had not been built.

The eventual choice of Waltham Forest Council was a scheme prepared by the Heron Property Corporation and in 1985 work commenced, being completed in 1988 when the Selborne Walk Shopping Centre was opened. One of the conditions of awarding the contract was an obligation placed on the developer to provide some facility for public use, other than shops or commercial premises, to compensate for the loss of some then existing services. As previously noted, the project accepted by the Council was the provision of a much needed extension to the Central Library with an open 'piazza' area adjacent to the building. Another requirement was that the new buildings should blend in texture and height with the existing mainly brick built two or three-storey buildings along the street. As a result the Borough was spared yet another bland concrete and glass shopping precinct similar to many others in the country. In addition to these requirements the developers had to redesign and resite the bus station as part of the complete deal.

The main aim of the Council was to retain as much of the street market as possible and this goal seems to have been achieved. Amplified pop music may have replaced the itinerant bands, the players of spoons and piano accordionists, that previously provided a musical accompaniment to shopping, but the patter of the stallholders is still as lively as before. Magic liquids to turn brassware into chrome are no longer sold, and quack doctors offering "pills to cure all ills" are unlikely to flourish in the age of the N.H.S. Instead spare parts of once luxury goods such as vacuum cleaners or washing machines dangle from stalls looking almost like the intestines and appendages of early robots. Rows of 'designer' trainers fill stalls that once only sold prosaic black plimsolls. The fruit and vegetables on sale still make colourful displays but include fruits unknown to previous generations of shoppers to whom even grapefruit, let alone kiwi fruit, were undiscovered delights. Duvets, not flannelette blankets are today offered at "ridiculous prices" and CD's, tapes and LP's can be purchased rather than heavy fragile shellac 78's which, more often than not, were broken on the journey home.

Some may regret the passing of the previous street market atmosphere, seemingly forgetting the fights, the struggles to buy cheap meat late on Saturday nights, or the poverty which led to regular visits to Uncle's (pawnbrokers) to raise money to live on, so well recorded in 'Memories of High Street'.[9] It should also be remembered that in twenty or thirty years time the sights and sounds of today's market will be recalled just as nostalgically. This publication must therefore end by paying tribute to the many stallholders who, often well before dawn, go to market to obtain the fruit and vegetables they sell, those who travel to set up stalls, stand around in pouring rain, freezing cold and even, sometimes, blazing heat, to provide goods at fair prices and lively patter completely free. Those who manage and work in the shops also contribute to its continuing existence, albeit more quietly and less exposed to the elements. Due to the work of these men and women the 'History of High Street' will still need to be updated from time to time.

References

1 Walthamstow Board of Health. These local bodies were the precursors of the present Urban District - Town and County Councils having powers other than Public Health matters.

2 Strange, K. H., 'Climbing Boys', London 1982.

3 Batsford, M. E., 'Non-Conformity in Walthamstow'. 2 Vols., London 1977. Reprinted 2002.*

4 Pond, C. C., 'Walthamstow & Chingford Railway', London 1970.*

5 The 1851 census for Marsh Street reveals that a large household was kept by a Mr John Silver, a London Merchant, and his wife Sarah. They had 3 sons and 3 daughters, aged from 12 to the baby son of 9 months, employed a girl of 19 as a governess, who came from Leeds, and an elderly nurse (aged 70) who also came from Yorkshire. A local girl was employed as an under nurse, as well as a cook and two housemaids, a gardener and his wife. This household comprising of 16 people also had a 'pastoral gentleman' of 50 staying with them.

6 'Jerry' building. A term used to describe cheaply made buildings possibly a reference to the Walls of Jericho!

7 Wyld R. ed., 'War over Walthamstow'. First published 1945, reprinted by London Borough of Waltham Forest 1989.

8 Tonkin, W. G. S., 'Showtime in Walthamstow'. First published 1967 revised edition 1983. Reprinted 2002.*

9 Howes, J. W., 'Memories of High Street'. First published 1977 by London Borough of Waltham Forest, reprinted by Walthamstow Historical Society 1988 and 2002.*

* Publications of Walthamstow Historical Society, formerly Walthamstow Antiquarian Society.

Advertisement published in the Walthamstow Official Guide (Eighth Edition) 1937.